LEO THE LION'S GREAT ADVENTURE

KEVIN PIERCE

Dedication

To Cammy, Bradley, and Charlotte—your love and support make every adventure possible. I couldn't do anything without the three of you. And to all the little explorers out there, may you always find joy in discovering the wonders of the world around you.

Description of the Book

Leo the Lion's Great Adventure is a delightful tale perfect for young readers in K-3. Follow Leo, a curious and adventurous young lion, as he sets off to explore the world beyond his cozy jungle home. Along the way, he meets new friends like Gerry the Giraffe, Bella the Cat, and Pablo the Penguin, and discovers exciting places like the savannah, the busy city, and the snowy mountains. Through his journey, Leo learns that while the world is full of amazing places, there's truly no place like home. This heartwarming story celebrates the spirit of adventure, the joy of friendship, and the comforting embrace of home, accompanied by charming illustrations that will enchant and inspire young readers.

Once upon a time, in a lush, green jungle, there lived a curious young lion named Leo. Leo loved his home in the jungle, but he often dreamed of exploring the world beyond the tall trees and dense vines.

One sunny morning, Leo decided it was time to satisfy his curiosity. "I want to see the world," he declared to his jungle friends. "I want to know what lies beyond our home."

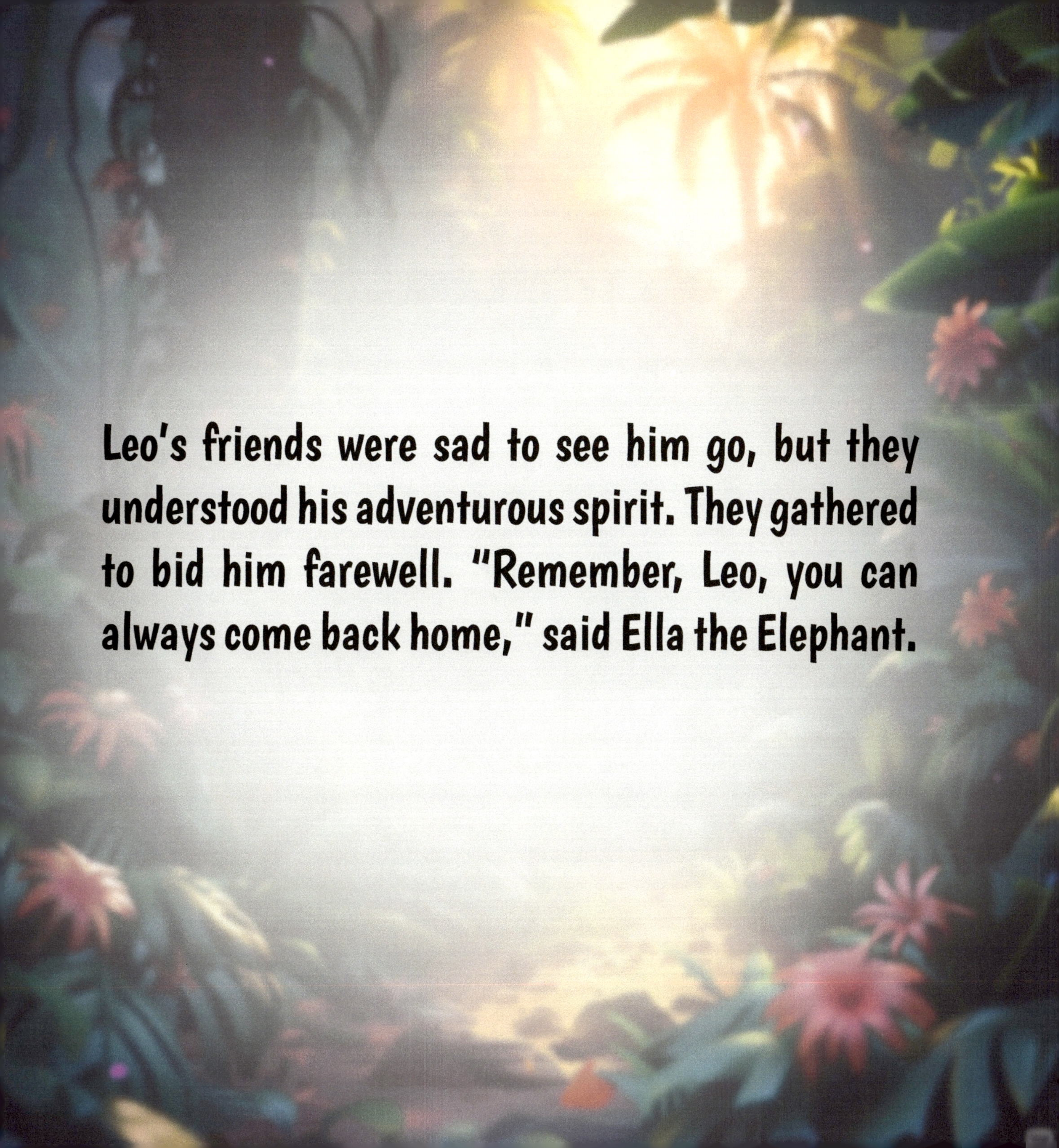
Leo's friends were sad to see him go, but they understood his adventurous spirit. They gathered to bid him farewell. "Remember, Leo, you can always come back home," said Ella the Elephant.

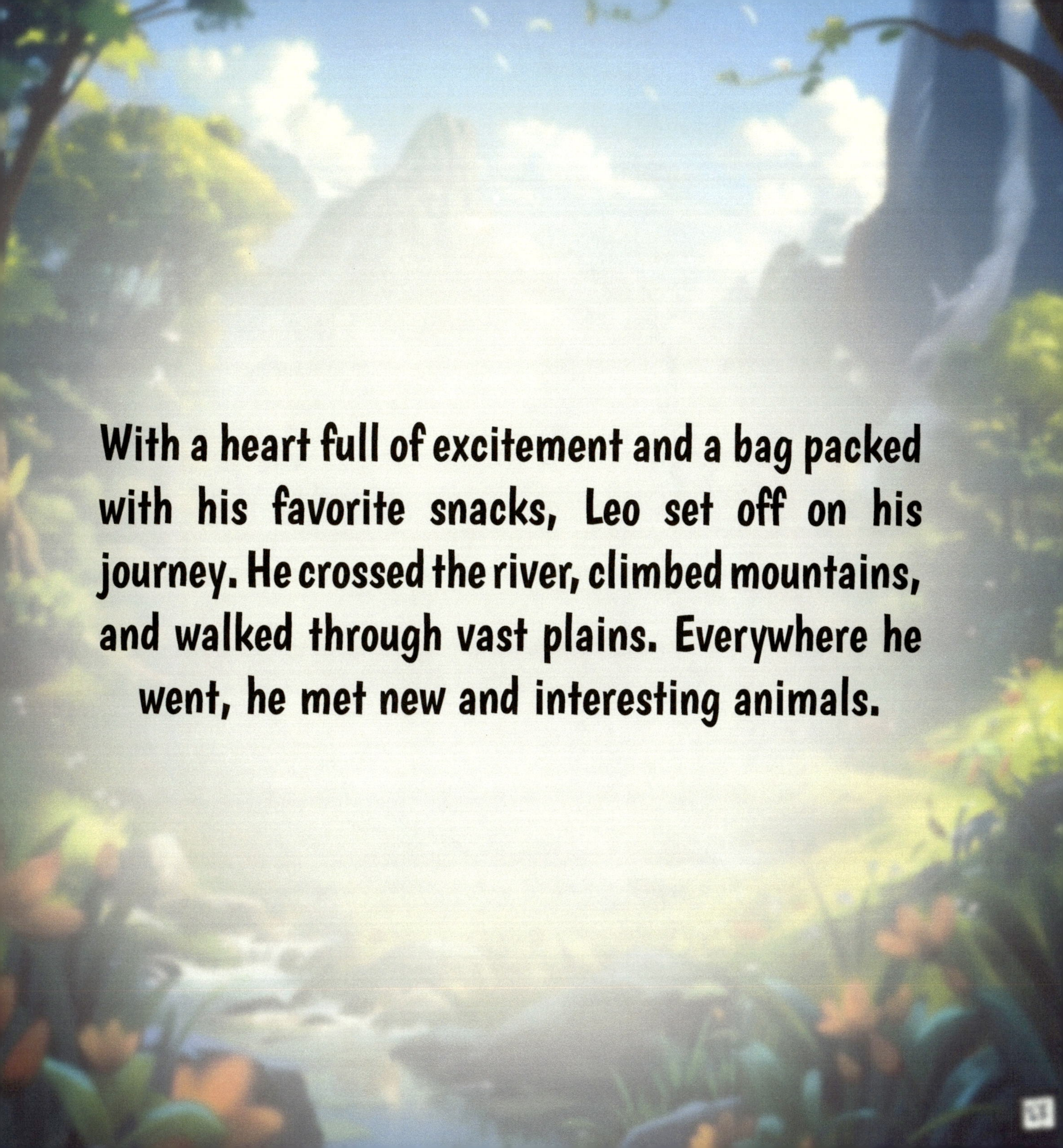

With a heart full of excitement and a bag packed with his favorite snacks, Leo set off on his journey. He crossed the river, climbed mountains, and walked through vast plains. Everywhere he went, he met new and interesting animals.

In the savannah, Leo met Gerry the Giraffe, who showed him how to reach the tallest leaves on the trees. "This place is amazing," Leo thought, "but it's so different from the jungle."

Next, Leo traveled to a bustling city, where he met Bella the Cat. Bella showed him tall buildings and busy streets. "This city is incredible," Leo marveled, "but it's so noisy and crowded."

As Leo continued his journey, he visited a snowy mountain where he met Pablo the Penguin. "This snow is so much fun," Leo laughed, sliding down the icy slopes. But soon he realized, "It's too cold here for a lion like me."

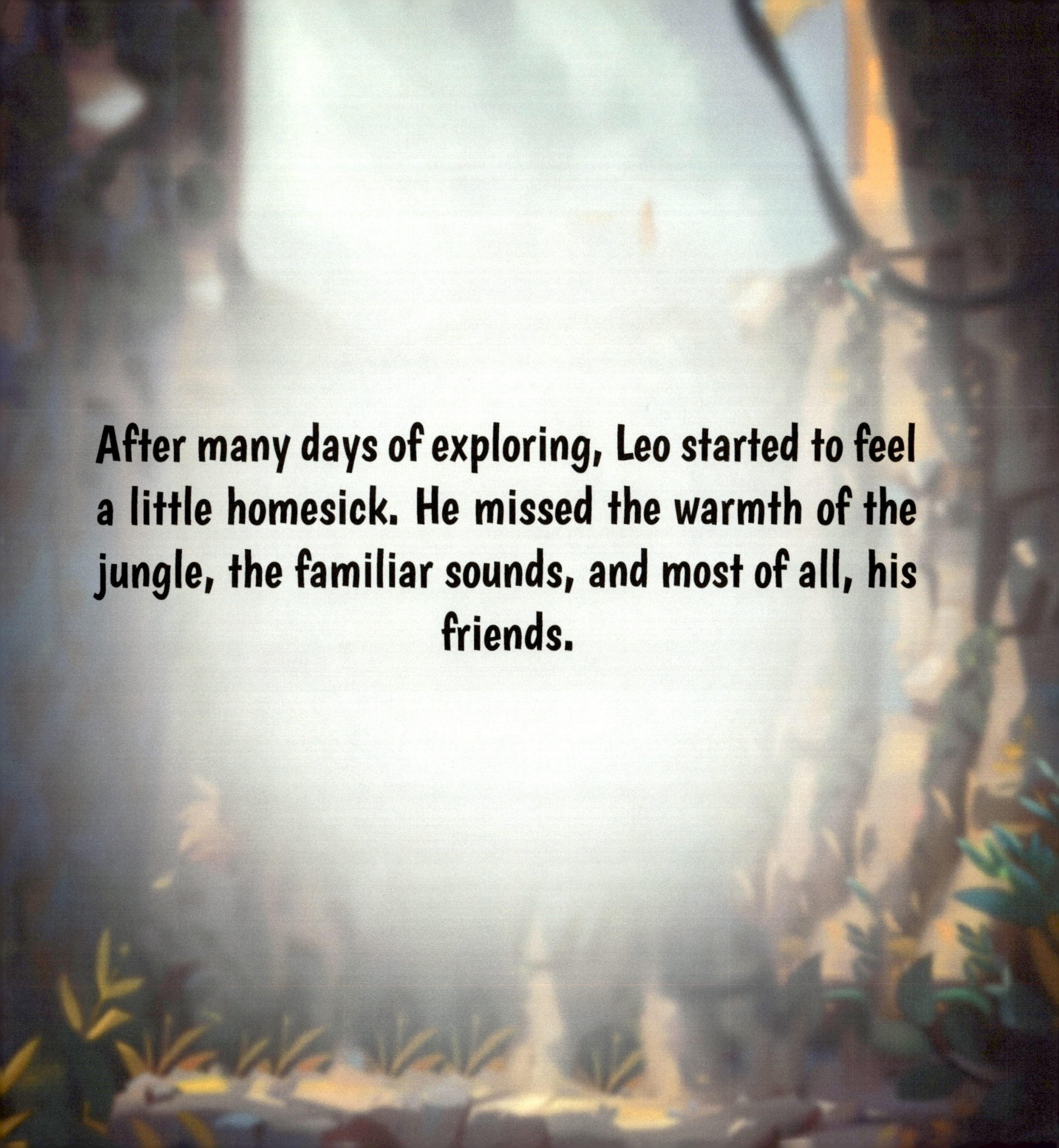

After many days of exploring, Leo started to feel a little homesick. He missed the warmth of the jungle, the familiar sounds, and most of all, his friends.

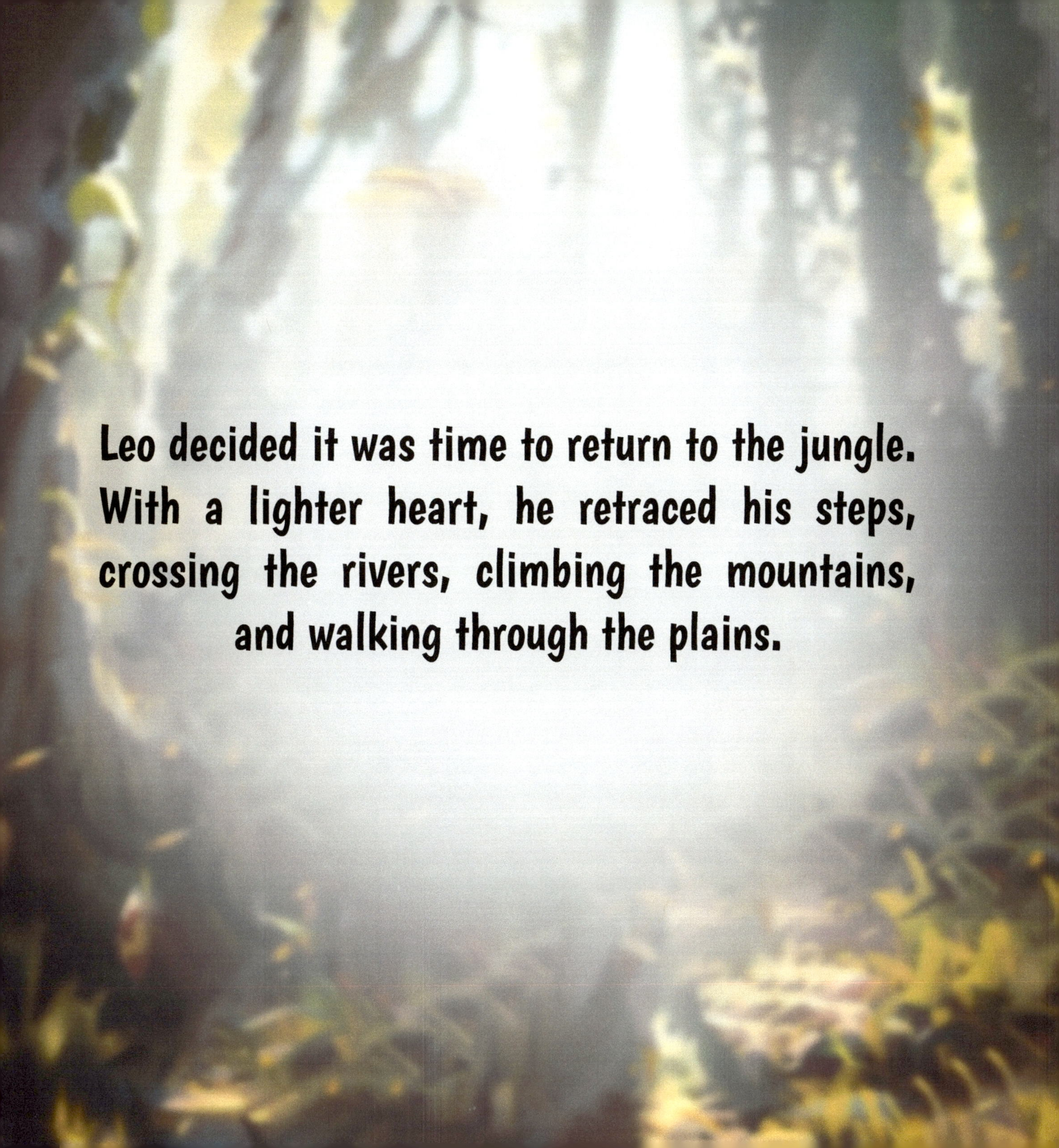
Leo decided it was time to return to the jungle. With a lighter heart, he retraced his steps, crossing the rivers, climbing the mountains, and walking through the plains.

When Leo finally returned, his friends were overjoyed. "Welcome home, Leo!" they cheered. Leo realized just how much he had missed his jungle home.

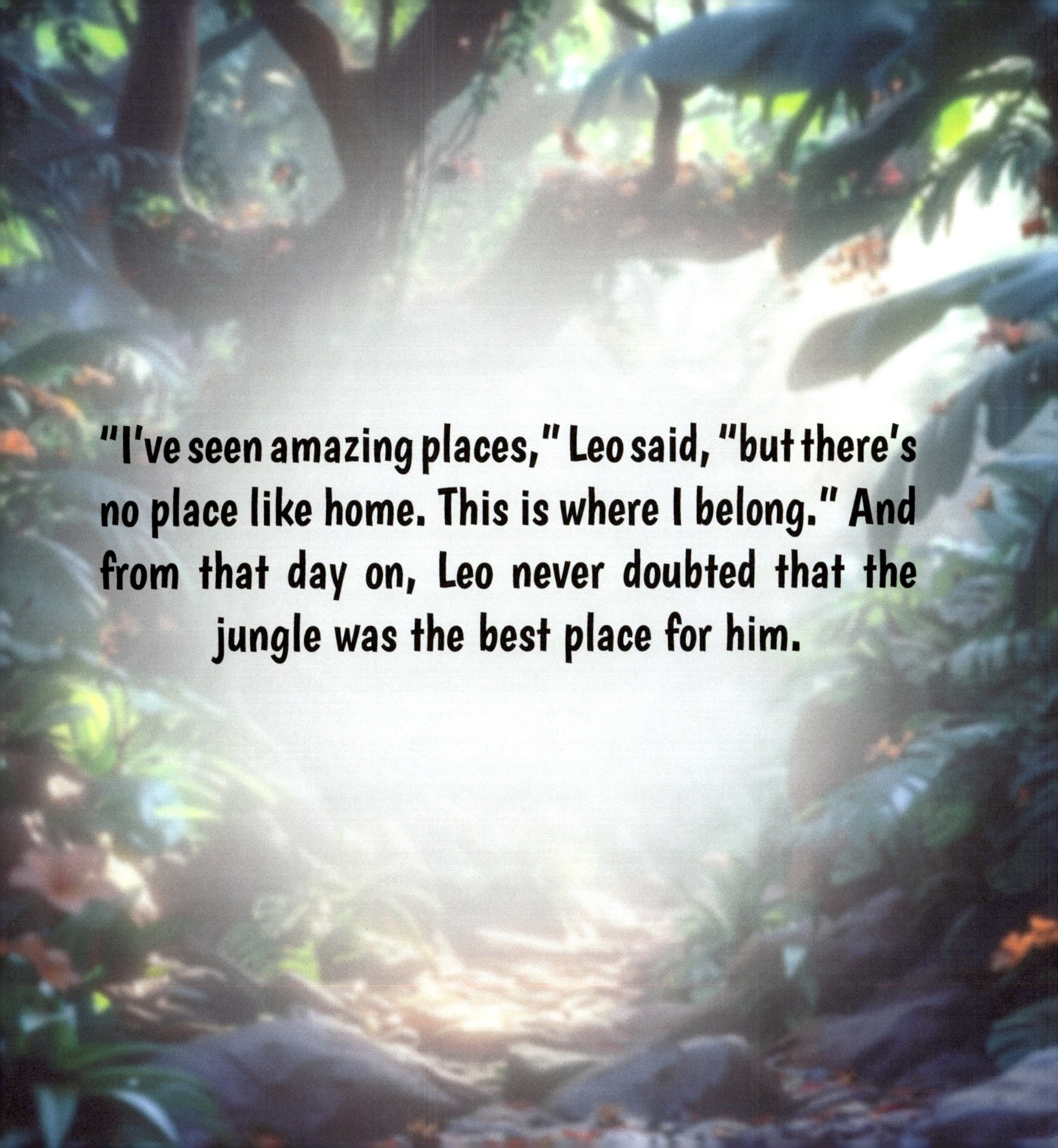

"I've seen amazing places," Leo said, "but there's no place like home. This is where I belong." And from that day on, Leo never doubted that the jungle was the best place for him.

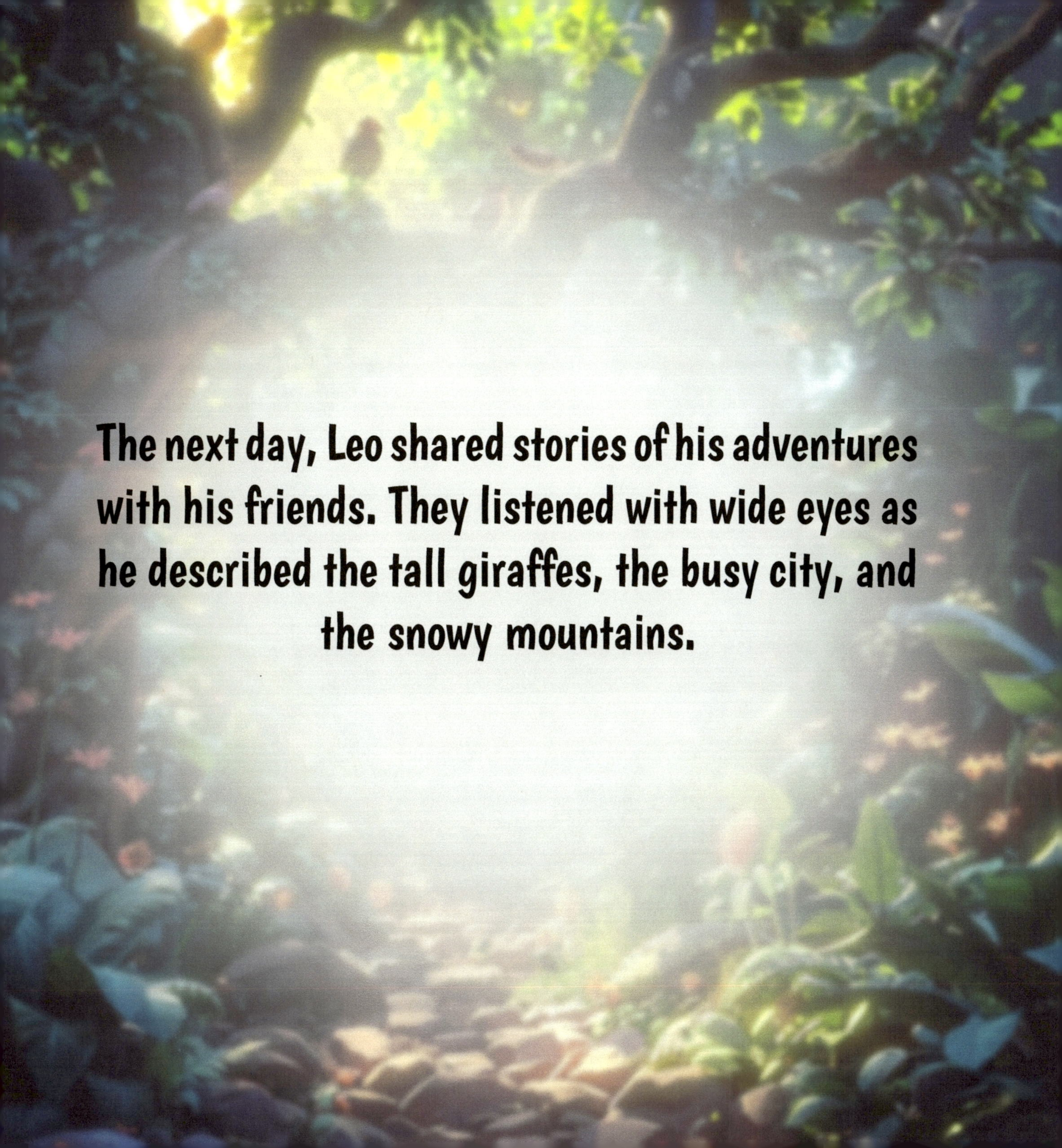
The next day, Leo shared stories of his adventures with his friends. They listened with wide eyes as he described the tall giraffes, the busy city, and the snowy mountains.

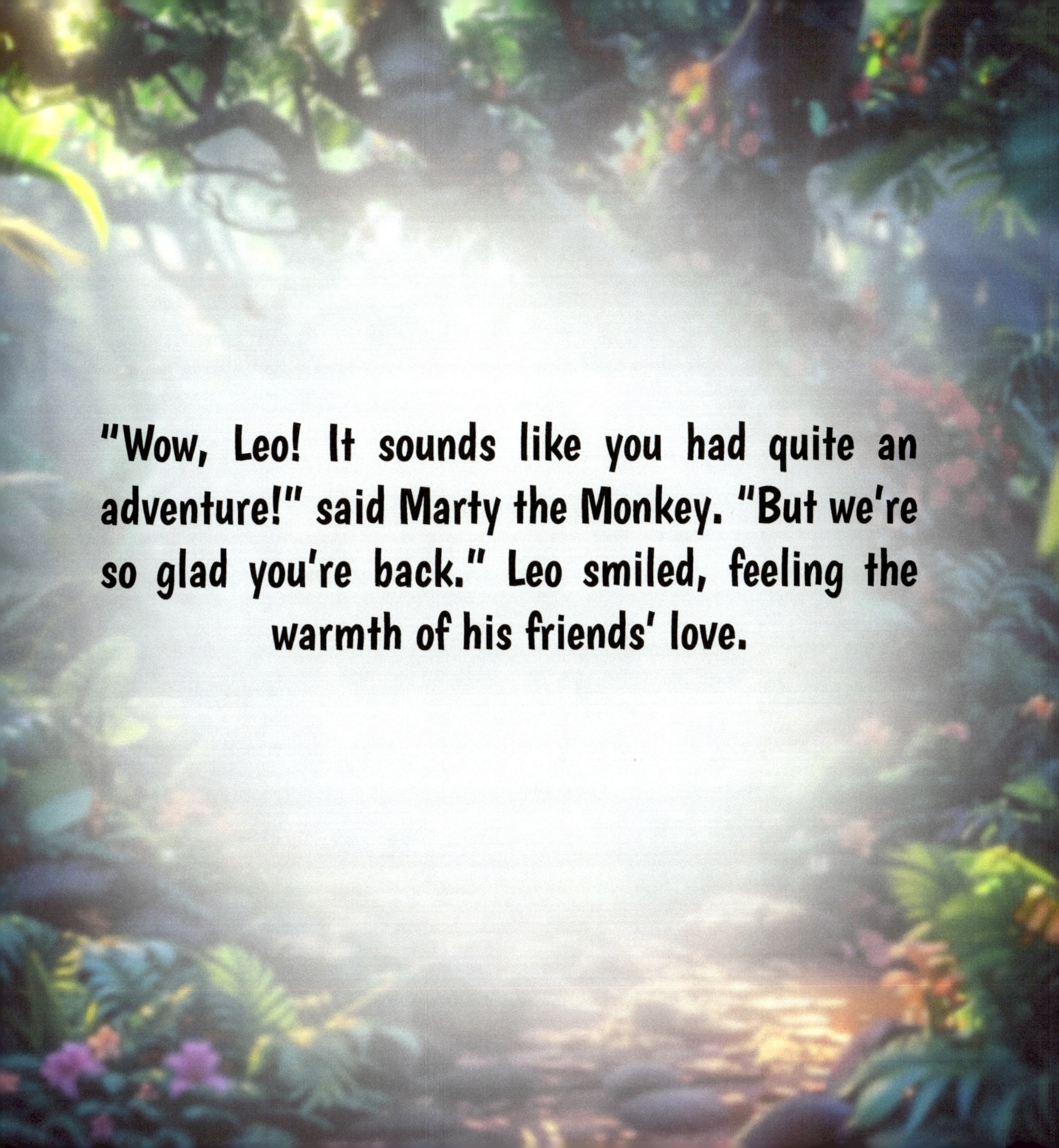

"Wow, Leo! It sounds like you had quite an adventure!" said Marty the Monkey. "But we're so glad you're back." Leo smiled, feeling the warmth of his friends' love.

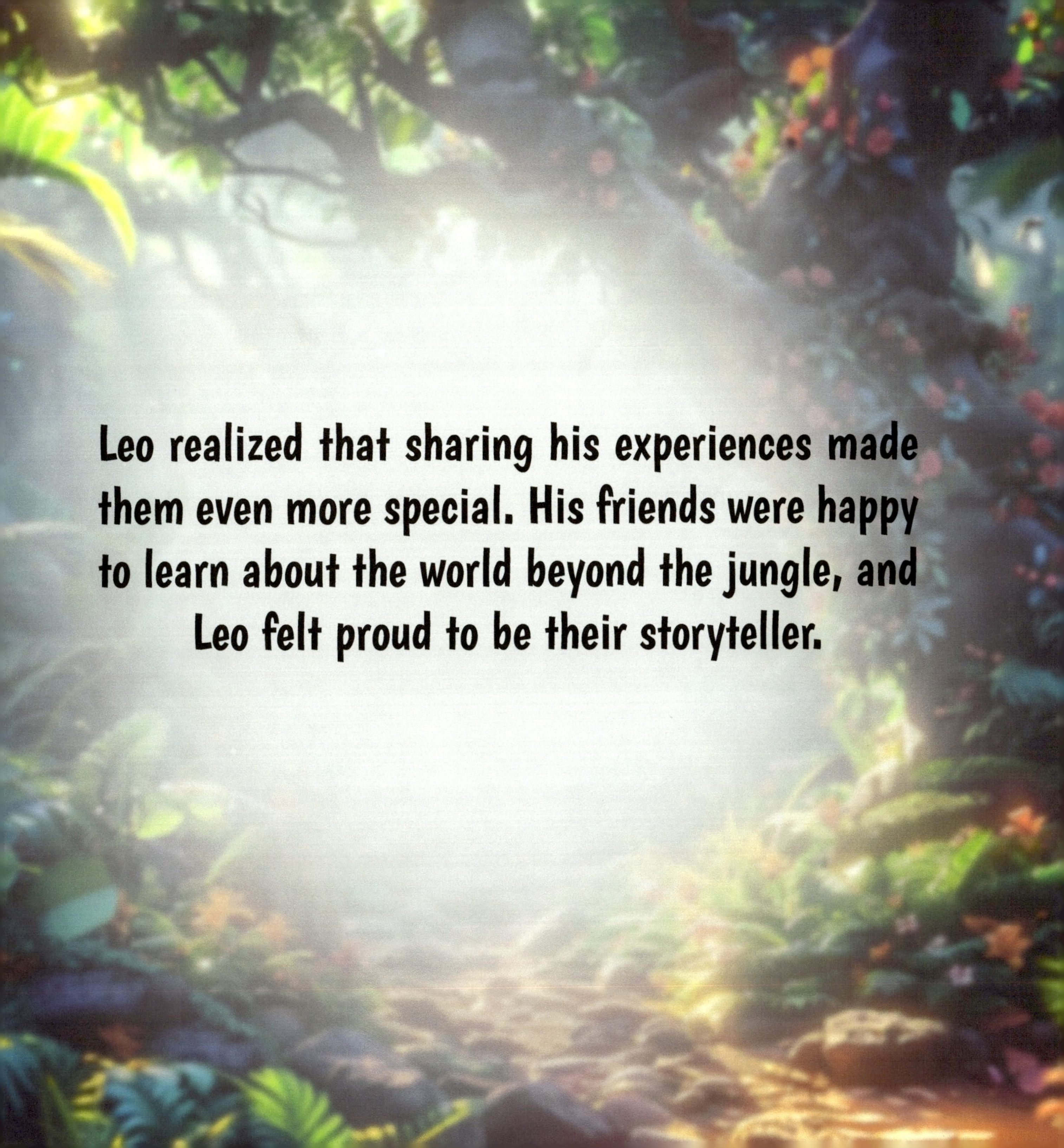

Leo realized that sharing his experiences made them even more special. His friends were happy to learn about the world beyond the jungle, and Leo felt proud to be their storyteller.

As the days passed, Leo and his friends played and explored their jungle home with newfound appreciation. They discovered hidden waterfalls, climbed the tallest trees, and watched the stars at night.

Leo learned that sometimes, you have to leave home to truly appreciate it. His adventure had shown him the beauty of the world, but it also reminded him that the jungle, with all its wonders, was the perfect place for him.

Leo the Lion lived happily ever after in the jungle, always cherishing his adventures but knowing that home is where his heart truly belonged.

Author Biography

Kevin Pierce is a dedicated educator, coach and storyteller with a passion for creating inspiring tales for young readers. With a background in teaching and coaching and a love for writing, Kevin brings stories to life that both entertain and educate. When not writing, Kevin enjoys coaching swimming, spending time with family, and finding new adventures to inspire the next story. "Leo the Lion's Great Adventure" is Kevin's latest book, aimed at igniting the imagination and curiosity of children everywhere.

Acknowledgments

A heartfelt thank you to everyone who made "Leo the Lion's Great Adventure" possible. To my family for their unwavering support and encouragement. To the talented illustrator whose beautiful artwork brings Leo's story to life. To the educators and librarians who inspire a love of reading in young minds every day. And to the young readers—thank you for joining Leo on his journey. Your sense of wonder and curiosity is the true inspiration behind this book